NATIVE AMERICANS
IN EARLY PHOTOGRAPHS

NATIVE AMERICANS
IN EARLY PHOTOGRAPHS

TOM ROBOTHAM

Reprinted 2004 by
World Publications Group, Inc.
455 Somerset Avenue
North Dighton, MA 02764
www.wrldpub.com

Copyright © 1994

ISBN 1-57215-353-9

Printed and bound in China by
Leefung-Asco Printers Trading Ltd

10 9   8   7   6   5   4

Page 1:
Crying to the Spirits
Edward S. Curtis
The Library of Congress

Page 2:
Little Big Mouth and Lodge, c. 1867-74
William S. Soule
*Smithsonian Institution National Anthropological Archives,
Bureau of American Ethnology Collection*

Right:
**Panoramic View of Buffalo Bill and His Indians
on the Beach in Front of the Cliff House, San
Francisco, California** (detail), n.d.
Photographer unknown
*National Museum of the American Indian,
Smithsonian Institution*

CONTENTS

INTRODUCTION

Europeans and white Americans since Columbus's time have been fascinated by Native Americans. Columbus himself wrote that the "Indios" he encountered were "so tractable and peaceable that . . . there is not in the world a better nation. They love their neighbors as themselves, and their discourse is ever sweet and gentle, and accompanied with a smile." The kindness and generosity of the natives did not, however, deter Columbus from enslaving them or from initiating policies that would ultimately result in genocide. But even as the subsequent expansion of white America decimated Native American tribes, many whites remained intrigued with their exotic ways and "primitive" nature.

It wasn't long before this intense curiosity sparked a demand for pictures and written descriptions of the natives. By the middle of the seventeenth century, narratives of captivity among Indians had become extremely popular. Indeed, according to literary historian Richard VanDer Beets, first editions of these narratives are now quite rare because they were "literally read to pieces." English artists, meanwhile, had begun to paint pictures of Native Americans as early as the sixteenth century. Many of these paintings, such as the famous portrait of Pocahontas wearing English clothing as a sign of her "civilized" status, were done in England during visits by Indians.

Artists continued to paint pictures of Native Americans

throughout the eighteenth century. Some of the images painted during this period reflected the romantic notion of the "Noble Red Man," while others depicted Indians as treacherous savages. Either way, however, they were indicative of white America's continuing tendency to mythologize the people whose continent they shared.

In the early decades of the nineteenth century, this tendency began to change. Increasingly, as settlers rolled back the frontier and forced tribesmen from their homelands, educated whites desired a deeper understanding of Native American culture. And, ironically, the more white America established its dominance over the native population, the more this curiosity grew. By 1813, when the great Shawnee leader Tecumseh was killed and Indian resistance to white settlement in the Midwest was effectively eliminated, this quest for understanding began to take on a sense of urgency.

"In the room of fear," observed a New York minister in 1819, "should now arise a sentiment of pity. The red men are melting, to borrow the expressive metaphor of one of their most celebrated warriors – 'like snow before the sun'; and we should be anxious, before it is too late, to copy the evanescent features of their character, and to perpetuate them on the page of history."

Among those who shared the minister's view was Colonel

Thomas L. McKenney. Serving under four presidents as the Government's chief liaison with Indian tribes, McKenney was instrumental in bringing Indian peace delegations to Washington. Although these efforts did little to improve the plight of Native Americans, they did facilitate the creation of an Indian archive, a collection of items "relating to our aborigines. . . ." In 1821, when a group of Midwestern chiefs visited Washington for a series of treaty negotiations, McKenney commissioned the artist Charles Bird King to paint their portraits. Over the next two decades, King continued to paint Indian delegations to Washington. But beginning in 1832, his efforts were overshadowed by those of George Catlin.

Like McKenney and others, Catlin was motivated by an acute desire to depict "the living manners, customs, and character of an interesting race of people, who are rapidly passing away from the face of the earth . . . [and] who have no historians or biographers of their own to portray with fidelity their native looks and history." Catlin, moreover, wanted white

Left:
Two Young Girls, Laguna Pueblo, New Mexico, 1902
Dr. Philip M. Jones
Phoebe Hearst Museum of Anthropology, University of California, Berkeley

Above:
Keokuk on Horseback, 1835
George Catlin
Oil on canvas mounted on aluminum
National Museum of American Art, Smithsonian Institution

Right:
Three Yankton Dakota, 1857
Julian Vannerson and Samuel Cohner of the James E. McClees Studio
Smithsonian Institution, National Anthropological Archives

Americans to look at Indians anew – to forget the stories they had heard of "Indian barbarities" and rid themselves of "deadly prejudices . . . against this most unfortunate and most abused part of the race of his fellow man."

With this mission in mind, Catlin embarked in 1832 on a 2,000-mile journey up the Missouri River. During the trip, he encountered the Lakota, Blackfoot, Ojibwa, and Crow. Over the next five years he visited the Sauk and Fox, Winnebago, Seminole, and many other tribes, and by 1837, he had done more than 500 oils as well as countless drawings.

Throughout the middle decades of the century numerous artists followed in Catlin's footsteps in search of whatever "wild" Indians still remained beyond the frontier. And while few of these men were as dedicated or open-minded as Catlin had been, they managed to create a plethora of images to satisfy white America's curiosity.

Meanwhile, a new science of image-making was taking the world by storm. In 1839, six years after Catlin's first journey up the Missouri River, the Frenchman Louis Jacques Mande

Daguerre had announced a process whereby an image could be captured on a silver-coated copper plate. Like all new inventions, the daguerreotype had its drawbacks. For one thing, exposure times ran anywhere from 8 to 30 minutes. As a result, capturing any kind of image was difficult, and creating photographs that truly reflected everyday life was virtually impossible. In spite of these problems, the invention of photography astounded the American public, and people quickly recognized its potential.

With the introduction of the wet-plate process in 1851, pioneers of the art form began to develop that potential. Taking photographs remained an expensive, cumbersome, and time-consuming process for many years afterward. But early photographers somehow managed to overcome the problems, and images of interesting subjects – including Indians – soon began to multiply.

Ironically, as new images of Native Americans spread across the land, the Native American population continued to decline. Between 1822 and 1842, the so-called Five Civilized

Left:
Indian Encampment, Shoshone Village, 1860
Albert Bierstadt
Oil on millboard, 24 × 19¾"
The New-York Historical Society, New York City

Right:
Shoshone Warrior, 1859
Albert Bierstadt
Stereograph
The Kansas State Historical Society, Topeka, Kansas

Tribes of the East had been herded from their homes in the Southeast to Indian Territory west of the Mississippi. The winter of 1838-39 had been especially tragic, as the Cherokee were forced to march westward on what came to be known as the Trail of Tears. Before their journey was over, nearly 25 percent of the group had died.

Over the next two decades, the Indians of the Far West also felt the full impact of white civilization as discoveries of gold in California and Colorado encouraged hordes of adventurers to stake claims on Native American lands. In the process, the natives were cut off from food sources, exposed to deadly diseases their immune systems could not fight, and killed in battles. Thus in California alone, the Native American population declined from 150,000 before the first gold rush to 35,000 in 1860.

Realizing that the spread of white civilization could not be stopped, many Indian leaders agreed to treaty negotiations in Washington. Most of the earliest photographs of Native Americans were taken during these delegation visits.

The first systematic effort to photograph Native Americans, as Paula Richardson Fleming and Judith Luskey have noted in their book *The North American Indians in Early Photographs* (1986), was made during 1858 when approximately 90 delegates from 13 tribes traveled to Washington, D.C. Most of the photographs were individual portraits taken by Julian Vannerson and Samuel Cohner of the James E. McClees Studio. McClees quickly promoted these images as another important attempt to preserve a dying culture.

"To the student of our history, as additions to libraries and historical collections, and as mementoes of the race of red men, now rapidly fading away, this series is of great value and interest," wrote McClees.

In addition to the work of McClees and his associates, Mathew Brady, operating out of a new Washington studio managed by Alexander Gardner, took a number of group portraits of the visiting Native Americans.

During the early 1860s, some photographers also traveled west of the Mississippi in search of Indian subjects. Joel Emmons Whitney, for instance, took numerous photographs of Sioux warriors after they had been imprisoned at Fort Snelling, Minnesota, for their role in the 1862 Sioux uprising.

Another photographer of frontier Indians during this period was the painter Albert Bierstadt. Traveling into the Rockies with a road-improvement expedition in 1859, Bierstadt gathered a wealth of material for the massive landscape paintings that would soon make him famous. In addition to sketches, this material included a series of stereographs – two photographic images of a single scene that were mounted in a device called a stereoscope to create the illusion of three dimensions. Many of these photographs featured Indians or Indian-related subjects, foreshadowing Bierstadt's lifelong interest in Native American culture.

The efforts of men like Bierstadt and Whitney notwithstanding, most of the important photography during the early 1860s took place on the battlefields and in the campgrounds of the Civil War. Indeed, these battlefields and encampments served as training grounds for many photographers who would later travel to the frontier and achieve significant recognition for their pictures of Indians. Moreover, as historian Lee Clark Mitchell has noted in his book *Witnesses to a Vanishing America: The Nineteenth-Century Response* (1982), wartime improvements transformed the camera into an efficient and reliable instrument. Thus when the war ended, efforts to photograph the Indian resumed with more fervor than ever.

In 1867, numerous Native American delegations again traveled to Washington, and several leading photographers were on hand to record the historic occasion. Gardner, who had taken some of the finest pictures of the Civil War, was

Left:
Alexander Gardner (left) with his horse-drawn photographic supply wagon while traveling west to photograph Native Americans in their homelands. (*The Bettmann Archive, New York*)

Below:
Indian Village Near Fort Laramie, 1868
Alexander Gardner
The Missouri Historical Society

among those who photographed this new round of treaty negotiations, and he again demonstrated his superior skills. As Fleming has noted, his group portraits were posed to record the most significant aspects of each occasion. In many cases, therefore, they are of greater historical interest than the individual portraits taken by Vannerson and others.

Gardner, moreover, was not content to wait for Indians to come to Washington. In 1868, he secured the job as Government photographer for another round of treaty negotiations – this time at Fort Laramie, Wyoming. He returned with a number of important photographs documenting meetings with the Cheyenne, Arapaho, and Oglala Dakota tribes.

Other post-war photographers were even more adventurous. Indeed, some of the most interesting photographs taken in the late 1860s and 1870s were shot by photographers who had traveled to the frontier – either privately or with government surveys – in an effort to capture images of Indians in their homelands. Three of the most important survey photographers of this period were Timothy O'Sullivan, William Henry Jackson, and John K. Hillers.

O'Sullivan, who had apprenticed under Mathew Brady and later worked for Alexander Gardner, was the chief photographer on two post-war surveys. The first, which began in 1867 under the direction of geologist Clarence King, afforded O'Sullivan excellent opportunities to explore Nevada and Utah. But it was with the second survey, which started four years later under the leadership of Army Lieutenant George Montague Wheeler, that O'Sullivan took his most important photographs. The year 1873 was especially productive, as O'Sullivan encountered numerous Apache, Hopi, Zuni, and Navaho tribesmen. By 1875, he had produced more than 2,500 prints.

John K. Hillers, meanwhile, was doing equally extensive work with the Powell Survey, led by Illinois geologist John Wesley Powell. After serving in the Civil War, Powell began exploring the mountains of Colorado in search of areas of geological interest. In the process, he came in contact with many Utes and became interested in their culture. When presented with the opportunity to lead a Government-sponsored geological survey, Powell saw it as a chance to pursue that interest.

Hillers initially joined Powell as boatsman for a trip down the Colorado River in 1869, but after apprenticing under Powell's original photographer, E. O. Beaman, he became the survey's principal photographer in 1872. By the time the survey ended in 1879, he had taken some 3,000 images.

Another important post-war survey was that of Ferdinand Vandeveer Hayden, which began in 1870 and included William Henry Jackson as its chief photographer. Jackson, who was born in 1843, worked for a short time as a freelance photographer in Nebraska following the war, and it was there that he first photographed Native Americans. By 1877, having worked with the Hayden survey and on his own, he had compiled an extensive catalogue.

While Hillers, Jackson, and O'Sullivan were traveling with the surveys, other photographers went west on their own. William Soule, for example, had opened a studio in Pennsylvania shortly after the war. But when it burned down a year or so later, he departed for Fort Dodge and quickly began taking pictures of Indians in the region.

Another important frontier photographer was William S. Prettyman, a Delaware native who traveled west in 1879. After serving for a short time as an apprentice to Kansas photo-

grapher I. H. Bonsall, Prettyman opened his studio, and for the next 20 years he photographed numerous tribes on the Southern Plains and in Indian Territory.

The collection of photographs amassed by all of these men is impressive when taken at face value, but it is all the more noteworthy when we consider the difficulties they had to overcome. Not the least of these difficulties was a lack of cooperation on the part of some of their subjects.

Jackson recalled how, during one stay among Uncompahgre Utes at the Pine Agency in Colorado, none of the Indians would pose. "Nor would they permit me to use my camera from a distance," he wrote. "When I set up my tripod on a commanding elevation to take a panoramic picture of the whole village, three or four Indians detailed to get in my way. As I attempted to focus, one of them would snatch the cloth from my head, or toss a blanket over the camera. . . .

"After three or four days of organized opposition I gave up. I had got a few really superb negatives, and I could foresee only mounting trouble if I persisted."

Top: An engraving of Charles M. Bell photographing Ponca and Sioux delegates, September 10, 1881; from *Leslie's Illustrated Weekly.* (*Smithsonian Institution, National Anthropological Archives*)

Left:
Sauk and Fox in Front of Elm Bark Lodge, 1880s
William S. Prettyman
Smithsonian Institution, National Anthropological Archives

Toward the end of his stay, Jackson wrote, "a chief who rejoiced in the name of Billy visited me . . . to give me friendly warning: this country, regardless of treaties and boundaries, was owned by his people; it would be dangerous for us to proceed farther with my strange box of bad medicine; hunters who had destroyed their game had died; other men who had dug in the ground and took away their gold had also died; it would be better for me and my companions to return at once the way we had come."

The Utes' reaction was not unusual. Some Indians called photographers "Shadow Catchers," believing that photographs captured part of the subject's spirit. But fear of photography was by no means universal among Indians. John Mix Stanley, the official artist and photographer on an 1853 railroad-survey expedition, had an experience quite different from the one Jackson described. According to Isaac I. Stevens, the survey leader, the Blackfoot tribesmen photographed by Stanley were "delighted and astonished to see their likeness produced by direct action of the sun. They worship the sun, and they [believed] Mr. Stanley was inspired by their divinity, and thus became in their eyes a great medicine man." (Unfortunately, none of Stanley's photographs survived.)

As time went on, other Native Americans came to see photography as a means of documenting their plight. Un-

fortunately, many photographers of the late 1800s were not interested in straight documentation. White Americans wanted to see Indians as they imagined them to be, not as they actually were. Thus Hillers and other photographers sometimes posed and dressed subjects in a certain way in order to heighten the viewer's sense of romance. That the Indians they encountered were often far removed from the wild tribesmen of American mythology did not seem to bother the image-makers. Moreover, while photographers often selected subjects based on ethnographic value, they were at other times motivated by commercial considerations.

Not all photographs of the late nineteenth century were sentimental delusions, however. Some photographers staunchly resisted the trend toward romanticism in favor of a documentary approach. As a result, they captured on film a wide range of images, from ritual dances to harsh scenes of reservation life. The latter scenes were not, perhaps, what white Americans wanted to see, but they reflected the physical reality of Indian life.

Indian reservations, in a general sense, had been around for some time, but after the Civil War they were located on smaller, more remote desert or semi-desert tracts. Throughout the 1870s and early 1880s, meanwhile, professional hunters slaughtered an estimated 30 million head of buffalo, leaving the Plains Indians without a major source of food and clothing. Adding insult to injury, the white hunters often took nothing more than the tongues and the hides, leaving the carcasses to rot in the sun. The tribesmen, who used every part of the animal for food, clothing, and other purposes, were horrified.

Initially, when they were sent to reservations, Indians tried to retain a sense of their traditional life in a variety of ways. Some, for instance, insisted on being given live government cattle instead of meat so they could preserve the ritual of the hunt despite the decimation of the buffalo herds. Thomas J. Morgan, Commissioner of Indian Affairs in the late 1800s, eventually put an end to such imitation-hunts because he felt they were unsanitary and served to "nourish brutal instincts." Increasingly, whites forced Indians to give up all sorts of traditional practices on the premise that they encouraged savagery.

The emergence of schools designed to teach Indian children the ways of white culture reflected this belief. Established at the urging of a small but dedicated group of white Christians who called themselves "Friends of the Indian," the schools initially

appeared to be successful. Photographs, often taken by the teachers themselves, reinforced this impression by showing Native American children wearing neatly pressed uniforms and working diligently at some "civilized" task. Ultimately, however, whites had to acknowledge that the experiments in education had failed. The failure was due, in large part, to the fact that Indians simply did not want to become part of white culture. Indeed, when looking at these photographs today, one is struck by the sadness in the children's eyes.

A related attempt to assimilate Native Americans into white culture was made in 1887 when Congress passed the Dawes Severalty Act, also known as the General Allotment Act. The legislation converted all Indian tribal lands to private property, under the assumption that adherence to the "communistic" ways of tribal culture was preventing the Indian from becoming "civilized." Each Indian family was allotted 160 acres, while individuals were granted 80 acres. But the act had two stipulations. First, the Government would hold each allotment in trust for 25 years to give Indians time to learn to protect their property from shrewd whites who might try to take it away. Second, since the allotments, in total, did not equal the total acreage controlled by Indians at the time, all "surplus" lands were opened up for white settlement. Consequently, while the act was ostensibly passed for the good of the Native Americans, it resulted in even more land being taken away from them.

Left:
**Indians Killing and Cutting
Up a Steer**, 1868
Alexander Gardner
The Missouri Historical Society

Below:
**A Group of Omaha Boys,
Carlisle Indian School,
Pennsylvania**, c. 1880
J. N. Choate
The National Archives

While Native Americans held some 138 million acres in 1887, they had less than 78 million by 1900, and by 1934, when the act was reversed and tribes were again recognized, their land holdings had dwindled to 48 million acres.

The Government's unrelenting attempts to destroy Native American culture and its unwillingness to ensure decent living conditions on reservations brought a variety of responses from tribal groups in the last decades of the nineteenth century. Some fled to Mexico or Canada, while others tried to adjust to reservation life as best they could. Increasingly, however, the Army reacted violently to even the smallest signs of protest. Such was the case in December 1890 at Wounded Knee Creek in South Dakota.

The trouble began in the late fall when the cult of the Ghost Dance spread rapidly across Sioux reservations. The cult was wholly non-violent, but whites who witnessed its ritual dance were nonetheless terrified, and they moved quickly to arrest those believed to be responsible for the "disturbances."

In late December, after Sitting Bull was killed during a confrontation with soldiers, the Army moved to arrest Big Foot, another alleged instigator. Upon learning of Sitting Bull's death, Big Foot and his band of Minneconjou departed for the Pine Ridge Reservation, hoping to find safety in the camp of the great chief Red Cloud. Before he could get there, however, the Army intercepted him.

Big Foot, who was quite ill, immediately raised a white flag. Unfortunately, as the soldiers attempted to disarm the Indians, a shot rang out, and within seconds the soldiers began gunning down the Indians indiscriminately. When it was over, some 300 men, women, and children had been killed.

The first photographer to arrive at Wounded Knee Creek after the massacre was George Trager. His photographs, including the frequently reproduced picture of Big Foot's corpse lying in the snow, were widely distributed. Other photographers arrived afterward to document the horror.

As vivid as they were, however, these photographs could not convey the true significance of the tragedy at Wounded Knee: the days of Indian resistance to white settlement had come to an end. Indeed, that same year, the U.S. Census had declared that the American frontier no longer existed. Whites had settled in every region of the United States. The Native American population in the continental United States, meanwhile, had dropped to just 228,000 from a high of one to several million in pre-Columbian times. (Some estimates put the number at 1 million, others as high as 10 million.)

The final subjugation of the Native American gave rise to new feelings of ambivalence, guilt, and regret among many white Americans, and much of the photography that followed was as highly romanticized as some earlier paintings had been. One exception to this trend was the work of A. C. Vroman. In his diary, Vroman expresses deep respect for the Hopi tribesmen that he photographed as well as a sense of awe at the beauty of their costumes and rituals. As Susan Sontag has noted in her book *On Photography* (1977), however, his photographs are "unexpressive, uncondescending, [and] unsentimental." They are, in other words, true visual documents.

Other late nineteenth and early twentieth century photographers, the most notable of whom is Frederick I. Monsen, took a similar approach. But the style that ultimately prevailed among photographers of Indians during this period was that

Left:
Gathering the Dead at Wounded Knee, January 1, 1891
George Trager
Smithsonian Institution, National Anthropological Archives

Right: "The Club," San Juan Capistrano, California, 1900 (left to right) H. E. Hoopes, G. J. Kuhrts, A. C. Vroman (seated), H. I. Chatfield, unidentified. (*Seaver Center for Western History Research, Natural History Museum of Los Angeles County*)

Below:
Cañon de Chelly, 1904
Adam Clark Vroman
Platinum print
Amon Carter Museum, Fort Worth, Texas

Wanamaker elaborated on this point: "In undertaking these expeditions to the North American Indian, the sole desire has been to perpetuate the life story of the First Americans and to strengthen in their hearts the feeling of allegiance and friendship for their country."

Curtis, however, went even further. Indeed, not since Catlin had any one white man committed himself so thoroughly to the visual documentation of Native American culture. During the last decade of the nineteenth century, Curtis enjoyed considerable success as a photographer specializing in portraits of Seattle's social elite. The year 1900, however, would mark the beginning of his lifelong intense interest in the American Indian. Curtis's interest was piqued when George Bird Grinnell, a leading conservationist, invited Curtis to join him on a trip through Blackfoot country. The trip, according to Curtis's daughter, was the "pivotal experience" of his life. Indeed, the trip did not simply spark an interest in the Blackfoot. Curtis resolved in the aftermath of the journey to photograph all the Indian tribes west of the Mississippi.

Seven years later, Curtis published the first volume of a 20-volume photographic collection. In the introduction, he lamented the passing of Native American culture, just as so many of his predecessors had.

"The great changes in practically every phase of the Indian's life," he wrote, "have been such that had the time for collecting much of the material been delayed, it would have been lost forever. The passing of every old man or woman means the passing of some tradition, some knowledge of sacred rites possessed by no other; consequently the information that is to be gathered for the benefit of future generations . . . must be collected at once or the opportunity will be lost for all time."

By 1905, Curtis had achieved national recognition for what one critic called his "remarkable artistic and historical work." Among his admirers was President Theodore Roosevelt, who helped convince J. P. Morgan to underwrite the publication of Curtis's photographs. As a result, Curtis's reputation as America's premier photographer of Native Americans was secured.

In spite of Curtis's expressed desire to gather information for future generations, the photographs of this remarkable artist are not what they appear to be. By his own admission, Curtis attempted to depict Indians as they "moved about before [they] ever saw a paleface." To achieve this goal, he often posed his subjects in costumes that he thought were appropriate and in settings that seemed to him to represent days gone by.

Given the "artistic liberties" taken by Curtis, Dixon and many of their predecessors, it is sometimes difficult to look uncynically at early photographs of Native Americans. Indeed, even when there was no apparent tampering on the part of the photographer, one cannot help but feel uncomfortable with the notion, suggested by many of the photographs, that the subjects were exotic curiosities rather than men and women deserving of respect on their own terms.

On the other hand, it is clear that many photographers did

Above:
The Last Outpost, 1908-17
Joseph Kossuth Dixon
Smithsonian Institution, National Anthropological Archives

which is best exemplified by two photographers: Joseph Kossuth Dixon, and Edward Sheriff Curtis.

Dixon, who traveled between 1908 and 1913 with expeditions sponsored by department store heir Rodman Wanamaker, is especially important because he helped popularize sentiments about "the vanishing race" with a book published under that title. As Crawford R. Buell notes in his introduction to the 1973 edition of the book, Dixon's photography reflected a widespread tendency to "glamorize the Indian" out of desire to make "atonement for past injustices."

approach their subjects with respect. Curtis's dedication, in spite of all his faults, was especially remarkable. As Lee Clark Mitchell has noted, no painter or photographer before or after – Catlin included – collected such a wealth of ethnological information.

In the late 1800s, and even into the early decades of the twentieth century, such information was not easy to come by. Indeed, all photographers of Native Americans faced a daunting task, since the technology was invented at a time when unrestricted tribal life had all but faded into history. Because of this unfortunate timing, at least one historian has argued that early photographs of American Indians constitute "a visual record of a harassed, defeated, and degraded people." This is true, of course, but it is only a partial description. Many of the pictures reflect not only tragedy, but also triumph – the triumph of tribesmen who clung tenaciously to rituals, customs, and a sense of honor, in spite of all the changes they were forced to endure; and the triumph of those photographers who recognized this tenacity and integrity and went to great lengths to preserve it on film.

Below:
Three Chiefs, Piegan, 1900
Edward S. Curtis
The Library of Congress

Right: Edward S. Curtis in 1906. (*Special Collections Division, University of Washington Libraries, Seattle, Washington*)

THE EARLY YEARS

The earliest photographs of Native Americans sometimes disappoint modern viewers. We hope to get from them a sense of the vitality of nineteenth-century Indian culture, and instead we are struck by how stiff and unnatural the subjects look. Indeed, some of these photographs, like A. Zeno Shindler's 1867 image of Yankton Dakota delegates in a war-dance pose, seem almost absurdly at odds with the realities of Native American life.

The stiffness of these early images, of course, reflects the considerable technological limitations faced by early photographers. Exposure times were so slow, in fact, that portrait subjects often had to wear braces to help them keep still. Obviously, under such circumstances, photographs of a more expressive nature were not a possibility.

Given these limitations, it is remarkable that these mid-nineteenth century photographs hold any appeal for modern viewers, beyond their value as historical artifacts. But upon close inspection, the emotional power of these photographs does emerge.

The photographs of Thomas M. Easterly, who was among the first to work with Indian subjects, are good examples of how early photographers worked within the confines of the technology to produce portraits of subtle intensity. Easterly, a native of Vermont, moved to Missouri in the 1840s and began taking daguerreotypes of Sauk and Fox tribesmen in the region. Among the images that have been preserved from this period is the widely reproduced portrait of chief Keokuk, which was probably taken in 1847 in Illinois.

A decade earlier, both George Catlin and Charles Bird King had painted the chief's portrait. "Keokuk is, in all respects, a magnificent savage," wrote James Hall in the text accompanying the published lithograph of King's painting. "Bold, enterprising, and impulsive, he is also politic, and possesses an intimate knowledge of human nature." King's and Catlin's portraits both reflect this romantic impression. Easterly's daguerreotype, by contrast, is pure documentation. It evokes a profound sense of sadness, not because Easterly imposed his view upon the subject but simply because the camera lets us stare into the chief's expressive eyes.

Keokuk was originally chief of the Fox, a tribe that had remained at peace with whites throughout Andrew Jackson's campaign against the Indians. When the Sauk chief Black Hawk declared war on whites in 1832, the uprising was quickly suppressed and Jackson recognized Keokuk as chief of a united Sauk and Fox tribe. Subsequently, Jackson forced the tribe to relocate from Wisconsin to Iowa, and finally to Kansas. Keokuk remained on peaceful terms with whites until his death in 1848. Easterly, meanwhile, continued operating out of various studios in the St. Louis area until his death in 1882.

While Easterly was building his photography business in St. Louis in the 1850s, many of the century's most important photographers were beginning to do the same thing back east. Among the most important photographers of this group were James Earle McClees, Samuel Cohner, Julian Vannerson, and Marcus Aurelius Root, all of whom worked in Philadelphia.

In 1852, when a delegation of 19 Arapaho, Cheyenne, and Sioux traveled east for a visit with President Millard Fillmore and other white leaders, photographers seized the opportunity to record history in the making. Unfortunately, many of the photographs taken during this period cannot be credited to individual photographers with any degree of certainty. Nonetheless, it is safe to say that McClees and his fellow Philadelphians were involved in this endeavor.

A visit by a much larger delegation five years later marked the first systematic effort to photograph Indians, as Paula Richardson Fleming and Judith Luskey have noted in their book *The North American Indians in Early Photographs*. Among the most interesting images of this period is a portrait of the Mdewakanton Dakota leader Little Crow, taken in Washington by Vannerson and Cohner under the auspices of the McClees studio.

Like many other tribal leaders, Little Crow worked hard to maintain peace with the United States government. As Dee Brown noted in *Bury My Heart at Wounded Knee*, he even joined the Episcopal Church, built a house and started a farm after his visit to Washington. But by 1862, he was beginning to feel disillusioned. These feelings intensified when, in July of that year, thousands of Santee Sioux, including the Mdewakantons, waited in vain for money to which they were entitled under the terms of a treaty that Little Crow had signed.

In spite of his anger, Little Crow initially tried to calm his more militant followers. Some of the braves interpreted these efforts as a sign of cowardice, but the chief, as his son recalled later, insisted that the white man simply could not be beaten. The whites are "like locusts," Little Crow is reported to have said. "Kill one, two, ten, and ten times ten will come to kill you."

Little Crow was, of course, correct. Nonetheless, the chief eventually gave in to the cries for war and ordered an attack on the government agency that was responsible for the Indians in the area. When it was all over, 20 whites had been killed and the government warehouses had been emptied. During the following weeks, the warriors attacked several other white strongholds, including nearby Fort Ridgely, and in the process killed hundreds of people. But by late fall, the Santees had been defeated. During subsequent trials, more than 300 Santees

Sioux Delegation on Visit to President Johnson, 1867
Alexander Gardner
The Missouri Historical Society

were found guilty of participating in the uprising and were sentenced to death. President Lincoln later commuted most of these sentences, but the day after Christmas, 1862, 38 Santees were hanged.

Little Crow avoided the trial altogether, having escaped to Canada with a small band of followers. The following July, however, he returned to Minnesota in an effort to obtain some horses and was shot by bounty hunters. His son later learned that his scalp and skull had been put on display in St. Paul.

Six months after Little Crow's death, two other Santee leaders, Shakopee and Medicine Bottle, were also captured. For the next year they were held prisoner at Fort Snelling, Minnesota, but in November 1865, they were finally executed for their part in the ill-fated rebellion.

During their term of imprisonment in 1864, Joel Emmons Whitney photographed both Medicine Bottle and Shakopee. Whitney, a native of Maine, had gone to Minnesota in 1850 and learned photography under Alexander Hesler. His highly expressive portraits of the participants in the Sioux revolt are certainly among the finest of the period. In many ways they evoke the sense of melancholy that Edward Curtis would later try to convey. The difference was that Whitney's photographs were pure historical documents, whereas Curtis's were attempts to recreate the past. (See Chapter 3).

The horrors of the Sioux uprising were, of course, largely overshadowed for most whites by the Civil War. But when the war ended, the U.S. government renewed efforts to deal with the problem of white-Indian relations. In 1867, another wave of Native American delegates arrived in Washington, and a number of major photographers were on hand to record the meetings. Among them was A. Zeno Shindler.

Shindler, a native of Bulgaria, had studied painting in France before coming to America sometime before 1850. It is not known exactly when he took up photography, but by 1867 he was established enough to take over the management of McClees's Washington gallery. (McClees had actually sold the gallery several years earlier.) Shindler remained in Washington for most of the rest of his life, although he spent five years in New York and Philadelphia during the 1870s. He is also reported to have taken a trip west sometime during this period, although according to Paula Richardson Fleming, this report has never been substantiated. In any event, no frontier photographs have been attributed to him.

A more skilled photographer of the period was Alexander Gardner. Indeed, taking into account his extraordinary work during the Civil War and his later work on the frontier, it is safe to say that Gardner ranks among the greatest photographers of the nineteenth century.

What is most striking about Gardner's work is its range. Some of the studio portraits he took during the 1867 delegation visits are not significantly different from those taken by Shindler or any number of other photographers. But Gardner appears to have given more thought to composition than many of his contemporaries. His group portrait of a Sioux delegation with President Johnson at the White House is particularly striking. Moreover, in the years following the delegation visit, Gardner traveled west to capture images of Indians on their homelands.

Among the fascinating pictures taken during this period was his shot of an Oglala Sioux named Young Man, Even Whose Horses Are Feared, smoking a "peace" pipe during a treaty negotiation (see page 30). As Paula Richardson Fleming noted in *An Enduring Interest: The Photographs of Alexander Gardner*, this is the only known image of the pipe-smoking ritual.

Gardner returned to Washington after the Fort Laramie trip, and in 1872 he became the leading photographer of delegations. Ironically, although the government a year earlier had stopped negotiating treaties, 1872 would be an important year for delegation visits. Red Cloud, the Oglala Sioux chief, was among the most prominent delegates. "I want to be better acquainted with [the white man] and have a talk about many things," he said.

Several months after Red Cloud's visit, a Brule Dakota delegation led by Spotted Tail arrived in Washington, and Gardner took a number of important photographs of the group. His portrait of the chief's wife, taken during this visit, is among his finest studio works. Gardner photographed other delegations in 1873, but from 1874 until his death in 1882 he spent most of his time on other activities.

While Gardner was photographing delegations in Washington, another important photographer, William Soule, was hired by the U.S. Army to document the construction of Fort Sill, Oklahoma. The fort was deep inside Indian territory and thus afforded Soule an unusual opportunity to photograph the Kiowa, Arapaho, Apache, Cheyenne, and other tribes.

Meanwhile the careers of Timothy O'Sullivan and William H. Jackson were also beginning to peak. Their professional fortunes would be tied in large part to the Government's scientific surveys of the West.

As noted in the introduction, most of O'Sullivan's important work was done in the Southwest while he was traveling with the Wheeler survey between 1871 and 1875. The work was not only difficult, but also dangerous. Indeed, in November of 1871, several of O'Sullivan's companions were killed by Apaches as they were traveling by stagecoach to California. In spite of the danger, however, O'Sullivan managed that year to take hundreds of photographs of Mohave, Apache, Paiute, and Shoshone tribesmen. The two Mohave braves in the picture on page 38 were probably his guides.

In 1873, Wheeler appointed O'Sullivan "executive in charge of the main party," and it was during this period that he photographed numerous scenes of life among the Navahos near Fort Defiance, Arizona.

A decade earlier, the Navahos' life had been disrupted when Army troops under Colonel Christopher "Kit" Carson raided Canyon de Chelly, the tribe's traditional homeland in northeastern Arizona, and forced them to relocate to the Bosque Redondo Reservation in New Mexico. A new treaty in 1868, however, had allowed them to return to Arizona.

When O'Sullivan arrived, he found that he was able to photograph the Navahos engaged in a variety of traditional activities. One image, for example, shows a Navaho woman working a horizontal loom – a weaving method that was unique to the tribe.

While O'Sullivan was exploring the Southwest in 1871, Jackson was traveling farther to the north with the Hayden Survey. Among the Indians he encountered that summer was a family of the Bannock sheep-eater tribe in southern Idaho. Jackson later reported that the family agreed to have their picture taken in exchange for a small quantity of sugar and coffee.

The photograph of the Bannock family reflects their struggle for survival. Their primary food source, the bighorn sheep, was in short supply in the 1870s, and the Bannocks were, as a result, forced to wander about the region in search of sustenance. Many other tribes shared such an existence, of course, but few photographers captured the essence of that existence as well as Jackson did.

The Wheeler and Hayden surveys continued until 1879, as did the Powell Survey, which helped launch the career of John K. Hillers (see Chapter 2). But opportunities to photograph traditional Native American ways of life were rapidly disappearing. Increasingly, as Indians were forced to adopt the ways of whites, photographers faced new challenges. The various ways in which they responded to these challenges reflects the ways in which white America in general regarded the Native American in the last quarter of the nineteenth century.

Right:
Longhorn, a Sauk and Fox, c. 1846
Thomas Easterly
Smithsonian Institution, National Anthropological Archives

Left:
Keokuk, 1847
Thomas Easterly
Smithsonian Institution, National Anthropological Archives

Three Cheyenne Indians, White Antelope, Alights on a Cloud, and Little Chief, 1851-52
Probably by Marcus Aurelius Root or James E. McClees in Philadelphia
Smithsonian Institution, National Anthropological Archives

Above:
Little Six, Also Known as Shakopee, 1858
Julian Vannerson and Samuel Cohner of the
McClees Studio
*Smithsonian Institution, National Anthropological
Archives*

Left:
Petalesharo of Skidi Pawnee, 1858
McClees Studio
*Smithsonian Institution, National Anthropological
Archives*

**Cheyenne and Kiowa Delegates in the White House
Conservatory**, 1863
Photographer unknown
Smithsonian Institution, National Anthropological Archives

Medicine Bottle at Fort Snelling Prison, 1864
Joel Emmons Whitney
Smithsonian Institution, National Anthropological Archives

Above:
Yankton Dakota Delegates in Pose from War Dance, 1867
A. Zeno Shindler
Smithsonian Institution, National Anthropological Archives

Below:
Pawnee Men Before Earth Lodge, 1868-69
William Henry Jackson
Museum of New Mexico

**Young Man, Even Whose Horses Are Feared, Smoking Council
Pipe During Oglala Dakota Treaty Meeting at Fort Laramie,
Wyoming,** 1868
Alexander Gardner
Smithsonian Institution, National Anthropological Archives

Short Bull of the Sioux, n.d.
Photographer unknown
The National Archives

A Bannock Family in Medicine Lodge Creek, Idaho, 1871
William Henry Jackson
Smithsonian Institution, National Anthropological Archives

Wife of Spotted Tail, 1872
Alexander Gardner
Smithsonian Institution, National Anthropological Archives

Right:
Powder Face, War Chief of the Arapahoe, 1868-74
William S. Soule
Museum of New Mexico

Left:
Navahos with Horizontal Loom, 1873
Timothy O'Sullivan
Smithsonian Institution, National Anthropological Archives

Apache Desert Hunters Using Bows and Arrows, 1870s-1880s
Photographer unknown
Smithsonian Institution, National Anthropological Archives

Left:
Two Mohave Braves, 1871
Timothy O'Sullivan
The National Archives

Manuelito, Navaho War Chief, 1874
Photographer unknown
Smithsonian Institution, National Anthropological Archives

CULTURAL TRANSITIONS

The photographs of Native Americans taken during the last two decades of the nineteenth century reflect a culture in transition. Indians have been struggling with cultural change, of course, ever since their first encounter with whites. But whereas the earlier photographs tended to reflect these changes in very subtle ways, many of the images taken in the 1880s and 1890s clearly reveal the impact of white society.

One of the most interesting photographs of this period is a panoramic view of William F. "Buffalo Bill" Cody and the Indians who participated in his Wild West shows. Launched in 1883, the shows captivated audiences with colorful parades, exciting races, and elaborate reenactments of stagecoach robberies and Custer's Last Stand.

From a modern perspective, it seems curious that Indians were willing participants in these gaudy displays. But at a time when many tribes were barely managing to survive, opportunities to make money could not be taken lightly. Sitting Bull himself agreed to join the show in 1885, in exchange for $50 a week, a $125 bonus, and exclusive rights to the sale of his portraits and autographs, although he refused to participate in mock battles.

While most whites enjoyed these shows immensely, self-proclaimed Indian rights advocates were adamantly opposed to them. As one advocate put it, the shows "teach the Indian that what the white man really wants of him is amusement furnished by exhibitions of picturesque barbarism, not the acquisition of those sober, unpicturesque but absolutely necessary qualities which alone can make him equal to the battle of life. . . . "

In reality, many white Americans regarded the prospect of the Indians' cultural assimilation with profound ambivalence. Certainly most whites thought Native American culture was inferior to European-American culture. Nonetheless, many whites tended to romanticize the Indian. Their romantic attitudes toward Indian culture was expressed not just in their support of Wild West shows but in more serious endeavors to document traditional ways of life.

One photographer who recorded such traditional-looking subject matter in the early 1880s was John K. Hillers. As noted in the introduction, Hillers had established himself as a leading photographer of Native Americans while traveling with the Powell Survey. In 1879, Powell became the first director of the newly established Bureau of Ethnology, and he hired Hillers to be the bureau's staff photographer.

Under the auspices of the bureau, Powell organized an expedition to study the Indians of New Mexico, and by August Hillers was busy photographing the Hopi and Zuni pueblos. He returned to the Southwest again in 1880, and, with the help of Frank Cushing, a young naturalist who had gained the trust of the Zuni people, he was able to photograph many places and activities that would have been off limits to most whites.

While few photographers of the 1880s had the opportunities that Hillers had, he was not the only one to capture images of traditional Native American culture during this period. Ben Wittick, for example, took numerous photographs of Navahos and other tribes from his independent studio in Albuquerque between 1881 and 1884.

Another important independent photographer active during the early 1880s was A. Frank Randall. Working mainly in Arizona, Randall concentrated on the Apaches in the years leading up to Geronimo's surrender.

The Apaches had waged fierce guerrilla warfare against the U.S. Army for years, but in September 1872, the legendary tribal leader Cochise reached a peace accord with General Oliver O. Howard. When Cochise died two years later, however, younger Apache leaders, including Geronimo, resumed the guerrilla attacks. By 1880, when all other major tribes had surrendered to government control, Geronimo had become the principal warrior chief of the Apaches.

Geronimo's chief pursuer during this period was General George "Grey Wolf" Crook. In May 1883, Crook finally caught up with his adversary and convinced him to surrender. After spending two years on the San Carlos reservation, however, Geronimo fled once again, and it took Crook nearly a year to negotiate another surrender.

Camillus S. Fly, an Arizona photographer, was on hand to record the second meeting between the two leaders in March 1886. At one point, according to witness John Gregory Bourke, Fly "cooly asked Geronimo and the warriors with him to change positions, and turn their heads or faces, to improve the negative."

Crook was subsequently forced to resign after Geronimo broke the accord. By September, however, Crook's replacement, General Nelson Miles, captured Geronimo for the last time. Shortly thereafter, he was taken by train to Fort Marion, Florida. During the journey, he and a number of other Apache prisoners were photographed by A. J. McDonald of New Orleans.

Another Indian leader who attracted a following because of his disdain for treaties and reservation life was Sitting Bull, chief of the Hunkpapa Teton Sioux. During the 1860s, the principal leader of the Teton Sioux had been Red Cloud. But when the older chief signed the Fort Laramie treaty in 1868 and agreed to live on a reservation, his influence began to diminish, and Sitting Bull's dominance grew. In 1873, one of the major events of Indian-white relations was foreshadowed when Sitting Bull skirmished with a lieutenant-colonel named

George Armstrong Custer. Three years later, the Battle of Little Big Horn would turn both men into legends.

Following his victory at Little Big Horn, Sitting Bull fled to Canada, but in 1881 he returned to the United States and surrendered. Although he was initially imprisoned at Fort Randall, he was eventually permitted to live on the Standing Rock Reservation, and it is likely that this is where David F. Barry photographed him in the mid-1880s.

A native of New York state, Barry moved with his family to Wisconsin in 1861 and soon afterward met the photographer O. S. Goff. By 1878, he was managing Goff's studio, and the following year he took complete control of it. Throughout the 1880s, Barry took countless images of the Indians of the Northern Plains, and he developed a special interest in the Battle of Little Big Horn. His photographs of Sitting Bull are noteworthy for their simplicity.

Panoramic View of Buffalo Bill and His Indians on the Beach in Front of the Cliff House, San Francisco, California, n.d.
Photographer unknown
National Museum of the American Indian, Smithsonian Institution

Not long after Barry photographed him, Sitting Bull was killed as Indian police were attempting to arrest him. The government had grown angry with the Hunkpapa chief because of his support of what they viewed as a subversive phenomenon – the cult of the Ghost Dance.

The Ghost Dance cult took on many variations, but its basic premise was that a messiah had predicted the ultimate demise of whites and the restoration of the land as it was prior to Euro-

Masked "Mud Heads" Prepared to Dance, Zuni Pueblo,
New Mexico, 1879
John K. Hillers
The National Archives

pean settlement. The ritual's exotic nature naturally attracted photographers.

To George E. Trager, a Chadron, Nebraska, photographer, the commercial potential of the Ghost Dance was irresistible. He is reported to have made several trips to the Pine Ridge Reservation where Ghost Dance activities were concentrated,

although it is unclear whether he actually did make money from the photographs he took there. In any case, his efforts to capture images of the Ghost Dance were overshadowed by his own subsequent coup: Trager was the first to arrive on the scene after the massacre at Wounded Knee.

Trager's photographs were widely distributed, according to Fleming and Luskey, but his success was short-lived, and by 1892 he had apparently given up photography altogether. Other photographers, meanwhile, followed in Trager's footsteps, including John C. H. Grabill, who had been operating in Dakota Territory since 1886. In the long run, however, Trager's images were the ones that were generally associated with the tragedy.

The massacre at Wounded Knee was so psychologically devastating to Indians throughout the region that many people assumed it had put an end to the Ghost Dance. The cult had emerged, however, as an expression of hope against all odds, and the slaughter in South Dakota only heightened the need for such a ritual.

In an effort to understand the power behind the Ghost Dance, the government sent anthropologist James Mooney to investigate it. "The Indians are dancing the ghost dance day and night," Mooney wrote shortly after his arrival. "They are bringing out costumes not worn in years. . . . " Mooney was so swept up in the phenomenon that he continued to study it for the government and on his own for the next two years. In the process, he took a number of photographs of the dance as well as the only known image of Wovoka, the founder of the cult.

Activities such as the Ghost Dance, while fascinating to many white Americans, only strengthened the resolve of Christian reformers who were trying to teach "civilized" behavior to the Indians. Among the photographers who documented this effort was Jesse Hastings Bratley.

As a teacher at various Indian schools between 1893 and 1903, Bratley was in a unique position to document the assimilation efforts. The photographs he took at the Rosebud Reservation in South Dakota between 1895 and 1899 are especially noteworthy, but he also did important work at the Havasupai Reservation in Arizona.

While photographs by Bratley and others initially appeared to provide evidence of successful assimilation, enthusiasm for the schools waned as white America came to realize that these images were delusions. Indian children were indeed wearing uniforms and working diligently at assigned tasks, but ultimately they could not fully embrace white culture. As a result, they were caught in a kind of cultural void.

Over the next few decades, they would struggle to survive in this void. Some tribal groups clung to traditional ways of life, while others had no choice but to rely on meager government rations. Katherine T. Dodge's photograph of Apaches awaiting rations at the San Carlos Reservation is a poignant illustration of the latter. Such photographs made it increasingly clear to sensitive white Americans that the triumph of Manifest Destiny had its dark side.

Hopi Dance Rock and Kiva, Walpi Pueblo, Arizona, 1879
John K. Hillers
Smithsonian Institution, National Anthropological Archives

Approach to Pueblo Acoma, c. 1883
Ben Wittick
Museum of New Mexico

Left:
Hopi Woman Dressing Her Husband's Hair, 1880-82
John K. Hillers
Museum of New Mexico

Hopi Woman Dressing Hair of Unmarried Girl, c. 1900
Henry Peabody
The National Archives

Left:
Governor Ahftche of San Felipe Pueblo, Drilling Hole in Tortoise Shell, 1880
John K. Hillers
Smithsonian Institution, National Anthropological Archives

Navaho Man Hammering Silver, Another Using a Bow Drill, and a Child with Bellows in Front of a Hogan, 1892
James Mooney
Smithsonian Institution, National Anthropological Archives

**Crow Woman Decorating Staked and Stretched Buffalo Hides,
Montana**, n.d.
From Charles Rau Collection
National Museum of the American Indian, Smithsonian Institution

Navaho Silversmith With Examples of His Work and Tools,
c. 1880
Ben Wittick
The National Archives

Two Apache Babies in Cradles, Arizona, before 1884
A. Frank Randall
Phoebe Hearst Museum of Anthropology, University of California,
Berkeley

Right:
Nachez (Son of Cochise), Chief of Chiricahua Apaches, and His
Wife, 1882
From Williamson Collection
The Arizona Historical Society Library

"Nachez" "Nai-chi-ti" Son of Cochise & wife
Chief of Chiricahua Apaches.

Left:
Red Cloud of the Oglala Dakota, 1880
Charles M. Bell
Smithsonian Institution, National Anthropological Archives

An Apache Princess, Granddaughter of Cochise, c. 1886
Ben Wittick
The National Archives

Flathead Delegation 1884

No. 176—Council between General Crook and Geronimo.

COPYRIGHT 1886, By C. S. Fly. Tombstone, Ariz.

Left:
Flathead Delegation of Six and an Interpreter, 1884
Charles M. Bell
The National Archives

Council Between General George Crook and Geronimo, 1886
Camillus S. Fly
Smithsonian Institution, National Anthropological Archives

Left:
Geronimo, 1887
Ben Wittick
The National Archives

Marianetta, Wife of Geronimo, n.d.
Photographer unknown
National Museum of the American Indian, Smithsonian Institution

Apache Prisoners, 1886
A. J. McDonald
The National Archives

Left:
Sitting Bull of the Hunkpapa Sioux, n.d.
David F. Barry
National Museum of the American Indian, Smithsonian Institution

Sitting Bull's House and Family, n.d.
David F. Barry
National Museum of the American Indian, Smithsonian Institution

No 3609. "VILLA OF BRULE."
The great hostile Indian Camp on River Brule
near Pine Ridge, S. D.
Photo. and copyright by Grabill, 1891.
Deadwood. S. D

Camp of the Brule Sioux, Near Pine Ridge, South Dakota, 1891
John C. H. Grabill
National Museum of the American Indian, Smithsonian Institution

Right:
"Typical Home," Pine Ridge Reservation, South Dakota, 1891
John C. H. Grabill
National Museum of the American Indian, Smithsonian Institution

Part of the Ghost Dance, c. 1893
James Mooney
Smithsonian Institution, National Anthropological Archives

Big Foot's Corpse at Wounded Knee, January 1, 1891
George Trager
Smithsonian Institution, National Anthropological Archives

Dakota Girls Sewing at Indian Day School, Rosebud Reservation, South Dakota, 1897
Jesse Hastings Bratley
Smithsonian Institution, National Anthropological Archives

PL-232

Group of Students at Havasupai Reservation, c. 1900
Jesse Hastings Bratley
Smithsonian Institution, National Anthropological Archives

Group of Seneca, Cattaraugus Reservation, New York, 1900
Joseph Keppler
National Museum of the American Indian, Smithsonian Institution

Above:
Apaches Awaiting Rations at San Carlos, Arizona, 1899
Katherine T. Dodge
Smithsonian Institution, National Anthropological Archives

Below:
Salish Woman Smoking Salmon, British Columbia, n.d.
Photographer unknown
National Museum of the American Indian, Smithsonian Institution

Beginning of White Deerskin Dance, Hupa Tribe, California,
1890-97
A. W. Ericson
Smithsonian Institution, National Anthropological Archives

**Gable-Roofed House and Totem Pole, Bellacoola Village,
British Columbia**, before 1901
Photographer unknown
Smithsonian Institution, National Anthropological Archives

Kwakiutl Village, Hope Island, British Columbia, 1899
Photographer unknown
*Phoebe Hearst Museum of Anthropology, University of California,
Berkeley*

SUNSET OF A DYING RACE

When photography was developed in the mid-nineteenth century, people assumed that the camera accurately reflected reality. And often, it did. But as time went on, photographers of Native Americans increasingly looked for ways to "enhance" their images, either by adding costumes and props, posing subjects in particular ways, or "sandwiching" negatives for the purposes of adding dramatic backdrops.

After the turn of the century, this tendency toward embellishment was taken to new heights. Men like Edward Sheriff Curtis and Joseph Kossuth Dixon began to regard photography as an "art-science," and they unabashedly strove to capture the spiritual essence of the Indian rather than current, purely physical realities.

"The camera, the brush, and the chisel have made us familiar with [the Indian's] plumed and hairy chest," wrote Dixon in the 1913 edition of *The Vanishing American*, "but what of the deep fountains of his inner life? What riotous impulses, or communion with the Great Mystery, carved his face of bronze?" He went on to note that few scientists or artists had been able to shed light on these mysteries because "the inner Indian shrine is crossed by only a favored few."

Dixon counted himself among those favored few, as did his contemporary Edward Curtis. And like Dixon, Curtis believed his work revealed more spiritual depth than that of previous photographers.

"[T]he photographs are each an illustration of an Indian character or of some vital phase in his existence," Curtis wrote in the introduction to his book, *The North American Indian*. He added that in seeking "subjects of aesthetic character" he was not "neglecting the homelier phases of aboriginal life." But, in an effort to convey the Indian's true nature, he did indeed ignore the "homely" aspects.

Not all photographers of Native Americans in the early twentieth century produced such idealized images. M.R. Harrington, for example, traveled extensively in the East during the first two decades of the century and documented the gritty reality of contemporary life among the Seminoles and other tribes. Similar efforts were made by Alanson B. Skinner, DeCost Smith, and Joseph Keppler. But it is clear that the romanticized images of Curtis and Dixon, rather than Harrington's more journalistic photographs, reflected white America's sentiments about the "vanishing race."

As noted in the introduction, Curtis's early professional success was as a society photographer in Seattle. His love of the outdoors often brought him in contact with local Indian villages, and he occasionally photographed them.

Curtis's interest in Native Americans was heightened during an expedition to Alaska in 1899 with Dr. C. Hart Merriam,

chief of the United States Biological Survey, and Dr. George Bird Grinnell, an editor and authority on Plains Indians. Although Curtis took numerous landscape photographs during the trip, it was Merriam who took most of the photographs featuring natives.

The year after the Alaskan expedition, Curtis began taking more photographs of Native Americans. The best of these images earned him two first prizes from the National Photographic Convention. It was not until 1904, however, that Curtis began seriously contemplating his own "comprehensive and permanent record of all the important tribes of the United States that still retain to a considerable degree their primitive traditions and customs."

For the next two years, Curtis sought support for his massive undertaking, and he was largely successful in this effort. Ultimately, President Theodore Roosevelt himself took an interest in the project. But even more important than Roosevelt's support was that of J.P. Morgan. Curtis had approached the railroad magnate in 1906 with the idea of producing 20 volumes of ethnological text and illustrative photographs as well as 20 companion portfolios, each containing 35 large prints. Morgan was initially reluctant to offer his support, but after seeing the impressive body of work Curtis had already compiled, he decided to finance the project. It was the beginning of a 24-year effort that would eventually destroy his marriage, seriously endanger his health, and wipe out his finances. But Curtis's determination allowed him ultimately to complete the project: the last volume was published in 1930 when Curtis was 62 years old.

Curtis began work on the first volume in June of 1906, and his routine that year established the general pattern he would follow for the better part of two decades. The first five weeks were devoted to a general study of the culture of the Western Apache, and the remainder of the summer was spent actually taking photographs. The following fall was devoted to writing and preparing material for publication.

Volume one focused on the Navaho as well as the Apache, and Curtis was especially impressed with the tribe's crafts. A Navaho woman, he wrote, may not "write books, paint pictures, or deliver ringing addresses . . . but when, after months of labor, she finishes a blanket, her pride in her work is well justified."

This was no superficial observation. On the contrary, Curtis's comments were rooted in his extremely thorough study of the language and customs of the various tribes he visited. Nowhere was this dedication more evident than in his approach to Indian ceremonies. Not content to be a mere observer, Curtis would attempt to become part of the culture he

Lodge Interior – Piegan
Edward S. Curtis
The Library of Congress

was photographing. After repeated visits with the Hopis, for instance, he was finally able to convince the tribal priests to initiate him into the Snake Order so that he could actually take part in the sacred Snake Dance, a spectacular late-summer ritual that lasts nine days.

Curtis made comparable efforts to understand the rituals of other tribes, and such photographs as "Placating the Spirit of a Slain Eagle" reveal his empathy with the subjects.

While Curtis left no stone unturned in his research, however, he was quite selective in what he chose to publish. Any evidence of the impact of white society on Native American culture was generally removed. One picture of the interior of a Piegan lodge, for instance, shows a clock sitting on the ground. As Christopher M. Lyman has noted in *The Vanishing Race and Other Illusions* (1982), Curtis eliminated the clock through retouching before including a different exposure of this scene in *The North American Indian*.

By manipulating his images in this way, many scholars have argued, Curtis reinforced widely embraced stereotypes which survive to this day. But as Lyman notes, Curtis must be credited with artistic, if not scientific, integrity. Indeed, his entire body of work expresses a remarkably forceful and cohesive vision – one that is equivalent to a work of fine literary fiction. And fiction, after all, sometimes conveys a deeper truth than "fact."

Dixon, as already noted, took much the same approach, as the photographs in his book *The Vanishing Race* indicate. Published in 1913, the book was a report of the second of three expeditions sponsored by Rodman Wanamaker. The first, which traveled to Montana's Valley of the Little Big Horn in 1908, was undertaken primarily for the purposes of filming the movie *Hiawatha*, but Dixon took numerous still photographs as well. The second, in 1909, focused on the same region, but the objective was far different. This time, with an endorsement from President William Howard Taft, the members of the expedition would organize a council of Indian chiefs to record their recollections and attitudes in words and pictures.

Among those who participated in what came to be called "The Last Great Indian Council" were chiefs Plenty Coups of the Crow Nation, Timbo of the Comanches, John of the Apaches, Running Bird of the Kiowa, Brave Bear of the Southern Cheyenne, Runs-the-Enemy of the Teton Sioux, and Pretty Voice Eagle of the Yankton Sioux.

For the most part, these leaders were as enthusiastic about the council as its white organizers were. "I feel that I am engaging in a great work in helping to make this historic picture of a great Indian council," said Chief Two Moons of the Northern Cheyenne. "I·have led the Cheyennes in so many battles, and my life has been so full, that I felt when I came here that I was an old man. [B]ut since meeting the chiefs . . . and recalling my old life for this record, I feel like a young man again. It is a great day for all of us, because there are no more wars between us, and we meet in peace. . . ." The other chiefs made similar remarks at the closing of the council.

The success of his early efforts encouraged Wanamaker to take further steps to pay tribute to the Native American. In May of 1909, he proposed that a national memorial to the Indian be built on the grounds of Fort Wadsworth, Staten Island, near the entrance to New York Harbor. Congress voted to support the proposal, and in February 1913, the groundbreaking ceremonies took place. Unfortunately, World War I interrupted the project and it was never resumed.

As part of the ceremonies at Fort Wadsworth, the 32 Indian chiefs had signed an oath of allegiance to the United States. Several months after the ceremony, Wanamaker organized another expedition to bring a flag from the Fort Wadsworth site to 169 Indian communities, in honor of the Indians' becoming citizens. Since many Indians had been citizens for some time, the third expedition was received less enthusiastically than the second. Wanamaker and Dixon pushed forward with it nonetheless, and in the process added to the visual record of their great undertaking. In all, it is estimated that the Wanamaker expeditions produced approximately 11,000 photographs and 50 miles of movie film.

Looking back on the expeditions, Dixon imagined a time when Native Americans would have disappeared. "The door of the Indian's yesterdays," he wrote in his typically romantic style, "opens to a new world – a world unpeopled with red men, but whose population fills the sky . . . with sad spectre-like memories – with the flutter of unseen eagle pinions."

The irony of this view, of course, is that the Indian race was not vanishing at all. The Native American population had been decimated, to be sure, and it is easy to understand why the dying-race concept caught on in the early years of this century. Yet the descendants of ancient tribes have managed not only to survive, but also to hold on to some semblance of their traditional cultures. Theirs is, to borrow Dixon's words, an "imposing triumph of solitary grandeur sweeping beyond the reach of militant crimes. . . ."

Nez Perce Warriors, 1906
Major Lee Moorhouse
Smithsonian Institution, National Anthropological Archives

Blackfoot in Traditional Costume, Montana, 1903-10
Fred R. Meyer
National Museum of the American Indian, Smithsonian Institution

Right:
Angelic La Moose, Granddaughter of a Flathead Chief, Flathead Reservation, Montana, 1913
H. T. Corey
The National Archives

Left:
Very Old Chippewa Man in Traditional Costume, n.d.
From Fred R. Meyer Collection
National Museum of the American Indian, Smithsonian Institution

Seneca Eagle Dancer, Allegheny Reservation, New York,
c. 1905
M. R. Harrington
National Museum of the American Indian, Smithsonian Institution

Left:
Seminole Spearing Turtle in Big Cypress Swamp, Florida, 1910
Alanson B. Skinner
National Museum of the American Indian, Smithsonian Institution

Mandy Jumper, Seminole, Winnowing Corn. Florida, 1908
M. R. Harrington
National Museum of the American Indian, Smithsonian Institution

Last Family of Potters and Pipe Makers, Pamunkey, Virginia,
1908
M. R. Harrington
National Museum of the American Indian, Smithsonian Institution

Right:
Indians of Santa Clara Pueblo, New Mexico, Making Pottery,
1916
H. T. Corey
The National Archives

Left:
Sioux Maiden
Edward S. Curtis
The Library of Congress

Overlooking the Camp – Piegan
Edward S. Curtis
The Library of Congress

Cayuse Mother and Child
Edward S. Curtis
Special Collections Division, University of Washington Libraries,
Seattle, Washington

A Blackfoot Travois
Edward S. Curtis
The Library of Congress

X2759-08

Left:
Ready for the Charge
Edward S. Curtis
The Library of Congress

Start of a War Party
Edward S. Curtis
The Library of Congress

Above:
Coming For the Bride – Qagyuhl
Edward S. Curtis
The Library of Congress

Below:
Kwakiutl Masked Dancers in the Winter Ceremony
Edward S. Curtis
Phoebe Hearst Museum of Anthropology, University of California, Berkeley

Buffalo Dance at Hano
Edward S. Curtis
The Library of Congress

A Jicarilla Apache
Edward S. Curtis
Special Collections Division, University of Washington Libraries,
Seattle, Washington

Right:
Chief Joseph – Nez Perce
Edward S. Curtis
The Library of Congress

The Vanishing Race – Navaho
Edward S. Curtis
The Library of Congress

Right:
Praying to the Spirits at Crater Lake – Klamath
Edward S. Curtis
The Library of Congress

Skirting the Skyline, 1908-17
Joseph Kossuth Dixon
Smithsonian Institution, National Anthropological Archives

War Memories, 1908-17
Joseph Kossuth Dixon
Smithsonian Institution, National Anthropological Archives

Right:
Sunset of a Dying Race, 1908-17
Joseph Kossuth Dixon
Smithsonian Institution, National Anthropological Archives

LIST OF PHOTOGRAPHS

Select Bibliography
Belous, Russell E. and Robert A. Weinstein. *Will Soule: Indian Photographer at Fort Sill, Oklahoma 1869-74.* Ward Ritchie Press, 1969.
Dixon, Dr. Joseph K. *The Vanishing Race: The Last Great Indian Council.* New York: Doubleday, Page & Company, 1913. Reprinted 1973 by The Rio Grande Press, Glorieta, New Mexico.
Fleming, Paula Richardson, and Judith Luskey. *The North American Indians in Early Photographs.* New York: Barnes & Noble, Inc., 1992.
Jackson, William Henry. *Time Exposure: The Autobiography of William Henry Jackson.* New York: G.P. Putnam & Sons, 1940.
Lyman, Christopher M. *The Vanishing Race and Other Illusions: Photographs of Edward S. Curtis.* Washington, D.C.: Smithsonian Institution Press, 1982.
Prettyman, William S. *Indian Territory: A Frontier Photographic Record.* Selected and edited by Robert E. Cunningham. Norman: University of Oklahoma Press, 1957.

Acknowledgments
The author extends special thanks to Laura Nash at the Museum of the American Indian, Smithsonian Institution, New York, and to Paula Richardson Fleming, Assistant Director, National Anthropological Archives, Smithsonian Institution, for their invaluable assistance with this book. Thanks also go to Jean Martin, the editor; Rita Longabucco, the picture editor; and Sue Rose, the designer.